(NOT QUITE)

THE BIGGEST EVER TIM VINE

JOKE BOOK

THIS TIM VINE JOKE BOOK
BELONGS TO

....

(NOT QUITE)

THE BIGGEST EVER

TIM VINE

RED FOX

THE NOT QUITE BIGGEST EVER TIM VINE JOKE BOOK
A RED FOX BOOK 978 1 849 41620 7

Published in Great Britain by Red Fox,
an imprint of Random House Children's Books
A Random House Group Company

First published in 2010 by Century,
A Random House Group Company

This edition published 2011

1 3 5 7 9 10 8 6 4 2

The Random House Group Limited supports the Forest Stewardship Council (FSC®),
the leading international forest certification organization. Our books carrying the FSC
label are printed on FSC®-certified paper. FSC is the only forest certification scheme
endorsed by the leading environmental organizations, including Greenpeace. Our
paper procurement policy can be found at www.**randomhouse**.co.uk/environment.

MIX
Paper from
responsible sources
FSC® C016897

Red Fox Books are published by Random House Children's Books,
61–63 Uxbridge Road, London W5 5SA

www.**kids**at**randomhouse**.co.uk
www.**totallyrandombooks**.co.uk
www.**randomhouse**.co.uk

Addresses for companies within The Random House Group Limited can be found at:
www.**randomhouse**.co.uk/offices.htm

THE RANDOM HOUSE GROUP Limited Reg. No. 954009

A CIP catalogue record for this book is available from the British Library.

Printed and bound by CPI Group (UK) Ltd, Croydon, CR0 4YY

ABOUT THE AUTHOR

Tim Vine is a comedian. He was born in Cheam. He's a big fan of broccoli and darts and karaoke.

For my family, my friends and all of my fan

PREFACE

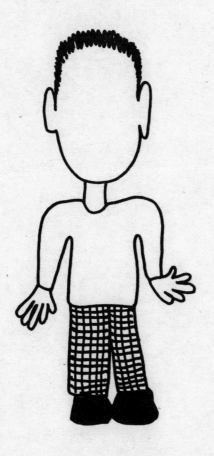

This bloke said to me, he said, 'I once got my dog to retrieve a stick from 100 miles away.' I said, 'That's a bit far-fetched.'

I don't like my hands. I always keep them at arm's length.

Dot dot dot. Dash dash dash. I really regret that. Remorse code.

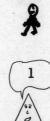

After I've had an argument I sometimes hold a Hoover over my head. It helps clear the air.

The other day I sat on a hairdryer. That put the wind up me.

I've got a friend who's a very tall blade of grass. He's easily swayed.

This bloke said to me, he said, 'I bet you can't name a famous Egyptian landmark.' I said, 'That's what you Sphinx.'

My dog's bark is worse than his bite because he hasn't got any teeth, and when he barks people's ears explode.

I saw a twenty-foot parrot the other day. You could knock me down with a feather.

I was adopted by a sports car. He took me under his wing mirror.

The other day I tied my head to a dog's tail. I just fancied a bit of a chinwag.

4

Conjunctivitis.com – that's a site for sore eyes.

I was watching a horror film and my skin peeled off my body and started tip-toeing round the house. I thought, This film is making my skin creep.

I saw this extinct bird with a hunchback. It was Quasidodo.

I didn't have a happy upbringing. I remember my third birthday party. I was fifteen.

Which of these two blueberries is the hardest to find?

I saw this angry verruca. He was on the wart path.

I spent the whole of today pruning. I was just chucking prunes at people.

My girlfriend is covered from head to toe in grass. Her name's Lorna.

So I went down the local hotel, and I said, 'Can you put me up?' and he nailed me to the ceiling.

This bloke said to me, he said, 'Why have you got manure on your head?' I said, 'I've just had my hair dung.'

What has lots of legs and a machine gun? A caterkiller.

I saw a coconut-flavoured biscuit playing football. It was Wayne Macarooney.

Exit signs, they're on the way out.

PASTA SAYINGS

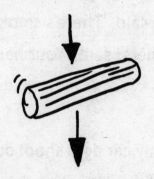

The Penne drops.

Black Beauty, he's a dark horse.

I've got a sponge front door. Hey, don't knock it.

I was working in a garage and Little Bo Peep walked in. She said, 'There's smoke coming out of my bonnet.' I said, 'Your hair's on fire.'

When I drive my car eggs shoot out the boot. It's a hatchback.

I'm colour blind but it doesn't stop me enjoying life. The other night I saw Joseph and His Amazing Brown Coat. It was great.

I was working in a health-food shop and this bloke walked in. He said, 'Would you like some Alpen?' I said, 'I suppose you think that's a muesli?'

So I got a job at Burger King and Andrew Lloyd Webber walked in. He said, 'Give me two Whoppers.' I said, 'You're good looking and your musicals are great.'

You invented Tipp-Ex – Correct me if I'm wrong.

So I was in the jungle and I saw this monkey with a tin-opener. I said, 'You don't need a tin-opener to peel a banana.' He said, 'I know, this is for the custard.'

This rabbit walked up to me. He said, 'Are you lookin' at me?' It was Rabbit DeNiro.

I was working in a travel agent's and this bloke walked in. He said, 'I want to book a flight, very short notice.' I said, 'You've just missed it.'

PARACHUTING MISTAKES

Canoe

He said, 'I want to go somewhere hot and secluded.' So I locked him in the photocopy room.

So I went to my GP and said, 'I feel like I've been hit on the head by a set of bongos.' He said, 'You've probably got slight percussion.'

The doctor said, 'You're turning into an airport.' I said, 'Is it terminal?'

I've got a horse called Treacle. He's got golden stirrups.

So I went down the local department store. I said, 'I can't decide whether to buy this bed or not.' He said, 'Do you want to sleep on it?' I said, 'Of course I do.'

I said, 'How much is it?' He said, '98.99.' I said, 'Make your mind up.'

I threw a stick in the sea and a round floating object brought it back to me. I said, 'There's a good buoy.'

15

SKI-JUMPER

Then a bag of cement went past at 100 miles an hour. I thought, That's quicksand.

I went to the doctor and I said, 'Why have I got crow's feet on the side of my eyes?' He said, 'There's a crow sitting on your forehead.'

So I went to the pants shop, I said, 'My name is Fronts and I want to put some pants on my head.' He said 'Y-fronts?' I said, 'None of your business.'

17

I said, 'I want to see some underwear.' He said, 'It's under there.' I said, 'Under where?' He said, 'I heard you the first time.'

I saw these two citrus fruits having a fight. It was Satsuma wrestling.

The other day someone burned the bottom of my shoes. It was soul-destroying.

My Christmas decorations are inflatable. I'm forever blowing baubles.

I refuse to work in a coal mine. It's beneath me.

I met a fox who was brilliant at football. It was Brazil Brush.

Actually my name isn't Tim Vine, it's Tim Buktoo. Sorry, I was miles away.

My local village was destroyed by toilet paper. Everyone was wiped out.

THE PROFESSOR SUDDENLY
REALIZED THE KNEE ON HIS
RIGHT LEG HAD REVERSED
ITSELF.

So I was in the party shop with my granny. She said, 'This kaleidoscope's rubbish.' I said, 'That's a balloon-pump.'

So I saw this dolphin serial killer. It was Jack the Flipper.

So I was on this train, I said, 'I don't think much of this bunk bed'. He said, 'That's the luggage rack'.

I went on holiday with my horse. It was self-cantering.

So I said to this bloke, I said, 'When I was on holiday I stayed in a bed and breakfast.' He said, 'Half-board?' I said, 'No, I was totally bored.'

I was a rubbish church window cleaner. I got rid of all the stains.

So I said to this bloke, I said, 'I'm going to North Africa.' He said, 'Tanzania?' I said, 'If I don't wear a hat it'll tan both of them.'

This bloke said to me, he said, 'You look like a medieval string instrument.' I said, 'Are you calling me a lyre?'

In 2002 the Queen had been on the throne for fifty years. Would JUBILEE vit?

I went down the local opticians. I said, 'Have you got a contact-lens solution?' He said, 'What about laser surgery?'

I went to school with a boy who had a concrete bum. When he got the cane, the teacher hit rock bottom.

I see the number of people doing the high jump has leapt up.

Did you know 30% of car accidents in Sweden involve a moose? I say, don't let them drive.

When I was offered a place at the College of Leapfrog I jumped at the chance.

I went down to my local town hall. I said, 'This town is in a mess, what are you going to do about it?' This guy said, 'Nothing.' I said, 'Why not?' He said, 'This is an aerobics class.'

Curries. Wouldn't touch them with a bhaji pole.

I just got a text from Heaven. That was a Godsend.

I came here on a sheet of sandpaper. It was a bit of a rough ride.

This bloke said to me, he said, 'Do you think there's life on Mars?' I said, 'Well, there's a couple of wasps round the wrapper.'

Last night I had a dream someone was saying 'On your marks, get set, go.' I woke up with a start.

I met a grumpy American. He was a Missouri guts.

So I saw this sad man in a refuse tip. He was down in the dumps.

I met a leech who was buying a Valentine's card. He was a sucker for romance.

This bloke said to me, he said, 'I'm going to be a chimney sweep.' I said, 'Soot yourself.'

So I said to Picasso, I said, 'Can you explain the out-of-shape faces?' He said, 'I think I'm about to sneeze.'

DOUBLE CHIN.

I went to the doctors. I said, 'I feel as though people can't see me clearly.' He said, 'Maybe you're a bit faint.'

Whenever I have a fight with someone I take a photo of it and put it in an album. It's my scrapbook. (I don't believe in fighting, by the way – it's just a joke.)

I'll tell you what often gets overlooked. Garden fences.

I've got a friend who used to hit fungus with a massive hammer. He really broke the mould.

Asthma. What a wheeze.

I know a woman who looks like a washing line. What's her name? Peggy.

I'm studying ceramics at the moment. It's driving me potty.

I went down the local fairground. I said, 'Coconut shy?' He said, 'Put it like this they don't go out much.'

So I went to the Tarot card reader, I said, 'It's my birthday today, can you tell me what the cards say?' She said, 'Sure – "To Tim, Happy Birthday, love from Granny".'

I left the fairground and I was beaten up by a local gang called the Hokey Cokey Gang and they all held hands and surrounded me. Then they put the left leg in and the left leg out, and they went in out, in out and they shook me all about. And every time I went 'Ohhh', they went, 'The Hokey Cokey'. And I thought, So that's what it's all about.

33

My mum said, 'I'm gonna dig a hole in the ground and fill it with water.' I thought, She means well.

I said, 'I'm going to buy a theatre.' She said, 'Are you having me on?' I said, 'I'll give you an audition but I can't promise.'

Then she fell on the floor so I rang up the hospital. I said, 'My mum's collapsed.' He said, 'Do you wanna stretcher?' I said, 'That'll make her feel worse.'

He said, 'What happened?' I said, 'A row of books fell off the wall and landed on her head.' He said, 'You've only got your shelf to blame.'

My father is a soldier. He's not a real soldier. He's a thin strip of buttered toast.

I went to school with a bloke who had two arms, two legs but no head. It was very strange when he did cartwheels because you could never tell when he'd finished.

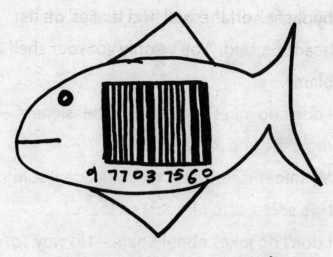

9 7703 7560

BAR COD

So I went to the doctors. He said, 'You've got hypochondria.' I said, 'Not that as well?'

I don't do jokes about graphic designers – I draw the line at that.

I don't do jokes about Spain – No way, Jose.

I don't do jokes about an elephant who's packed his trunk and left the circus– Not on your Nellie.

I went down the local music shop. I said, 'I want to buy a violin.' He said, 'Do you want to buy a bow as well?' I said, 'No, don't bother wrapping it.'

I got home and the phone was ringing. I picked it up and said, 'Who's speaking, please?' And a voice said, 'You are.'

So I rang up the local swimming baths. I said, 'Is that the local swimming baths?' He said, 'It depends where you're calling from.'

I said, 'Have you got a diving board?' He
said, 'Yes.' I said, 'Is it safe to use?' He said,
'No.' I said, 'Why not?' He said, 'It's nowhere
near the pool.'

I said, 'How deep's your deep end?' He said,
'Six foot.' I said, 'How deep's your shallow
end?' He said, 'Eight foot.' I said, 'How can
you have a deep end that's six-foot deep
and a shallow end that's eight-foot deep?'
He said, 'The deep end's only half full.'

40

JIGSAW PEACE

So I rang up my local building firm. I said, 'I want a skip outside my house.' He said, 'I'm not stopping you.'

This bloke said to me, he said, 'I'm a herald angel.' I thought, Ooo, hark at him.

One bruise plus two bruises equals three bruises. It's a lump sum.

One Pope plus two Popes equals three Popes. That's Catholic maths.

When I was young my mum, my dad, me and my brother and sister all wore one big woolly jumper. We were a close-knit family.

I'm very good at doing little spots with a paintbrush. I'm a dab hand at it.

I went to sleep with one eye open. I didn't sleep a wink.

I'm scared of cattle. I'm a coward.

43

SPOT THE DIFFERENCE

I know exactly when my friends are going to be sick. I'm a forensic expert.

Conjuring. That should do the trick.

I always say it's a marathon, not a sprint. That's why I lost my job as Usain Bolt's trainer.

Macdonalds was broken into twice today. It was a double cheese burglary.

Where do pigs do their Christmas shopping? Hamleys.

The Incredible Hulk's masseur. He always gets the rub of the green.

This bloke said to me, he said, 'Do you want to buy a barometer?' I said, 'I think I'll take a rain check.'

I can't remember my homing pigeon's name but I'm sure it'll come back to me.

Apparently Jupiter is the next big thing.

Legs up if you're double-jointed.

Did you know Peter Pan had a brother called Deep?

I've got a Christian mobile. It's pray as you go.

So I said to this anteater, I said, 'How do you eat flying ants?' And he just turned his nose up.

So I went down the local carpet shop. I said, 'Do you sell carpets by the yard?' He said, 'No, we sell them in here.'

So I said to Vincent Van Gogh, I said, 'Does having one ear affect you?' He said, 'Can you say that again I was only half-listening?'

I went down the local health spa and there was a sign outside which said COME IN AND BE PAMPERED. I walked in and they attacked me with disposable nappies.

So I went to the local karaoke bar. I said,
'Have you got "More Than Words"?' He said,
'Yes we also have music.'

I went to a country in the Middle East and
everyone was very boisterous. It was Rowdy
Arabia.

I've just got engaged to a girl called Ena.
Every time I see her I say, 'Hi Ena!' and she
laughs her head off.

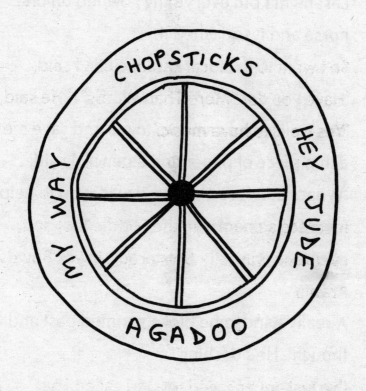

WHEEL OF 4 TUNES.

Last night I put everything I owned on one horse and it squashed it.

This policeman came up to me and gave me a thin piece of paper and a pencil. I said, 'What's that for?' He said, 'I want you to help me trace someone.'

A really handsome bloke sprinted past and I thought, He's dashing.

I went to the butcher's. He said, 'I bet you £10 you can't reach those two bits of meat.' I said, 'I'm not betting.' He said, 'Why not?' I said, 'The steaks are too high.'

Apparently 1 in 5 people in the world are Chinese, and there's 5 people in my family so it must be one of them. It's either my mum or my dad, or my older brother Colin or my younger brother Hochachu. I think it's Colin.

I always get very emotional when I go to weddings. The last wedding I went to I cried my eyes out. It was when the vicar said, 'I'm afraid she hasn't turned up, Tim.'

So I was getting into my car and this bloke said to me, he said, 'Can you give me a lift?' I said, 'Sure. You look great, the world's your oyster, go for it.'

Someone actually complimented me on my driving today. They left a little note on the windscreen. It said PARKING FINE. That was nice.

CAT   A LOG

So I went down the local ice-cream shop. I said, 'I want to buy an ice cream. He said, 'Hundreds and thousands?' I said, 'We'll start with one.'

So I went to the dentist. He said, 'Say "ah".' I said, 'Why?' He said, 'My dog's died.'

I was playing football on this aeroplane. It was amazing, I was running up the wing.

I'm on a special diet. I only eat things with the word 'special' in it. Special K, Special fried rice and, of course, Marks & Spencer's Strawberry cream sponge cake – on special offer.

I said to my German friend, I said, 'Why have you got a piece of meat in the boot of your car?' He said, 'That is my spare veal.'

You should've been at the manicure world championships. What a nail-biting finish.

IRON MAN.

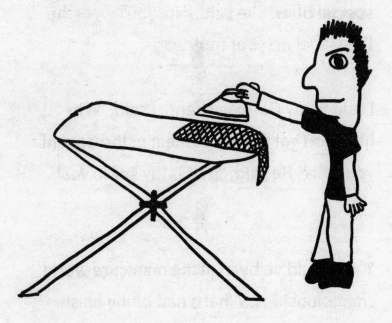

So I was walking down the street and this woman stopped me. She said, 'Excuse me, have you just washed your face with Imperial Leather soap?' I said, 'Yeah, can you smell it?' She said, 'No, you've got the little label on your forehead.'

You can't get Dairylea Triangles in Bermuda.

I bought some Bermuda shorts and when I took them off my pants had vanished.

So I went down the local garden centre. I said, 'I want to buy a garden.' She said, 'We don't sell gardens. We sell things that are in gardens.' I said, 'All right, I'll have a path.'

I rang up the local ramblers club and this bloke went on and on.

My dog's not very intelligent, he always misinterprets things that I say to him. I say 'Heel' and he goes down the local hospital and does what he can.

60

I got home and he was sitting on the sofa. I said, 'Get down!' And he started dancing.

When I meet someone called Angela I get a temperature. I think I've got Girl Angela Fever.

Did you know Demi Moore used to have a sister called Not Any?

I bought an exercise DVD. On the cover it said 'Running Time 75 Minutes.' I thought, I can't run for that long.

It's the fork that counts.

History. History. History. Yes, history repeats itself.

Tiddles stole my manure and I'm speechless. The cat's got my dung.

The traffic on the way here was so slow we were overtaken by someone going in the opposite direction.

This bloke said to me, he said, 'Have you ever kept a diary?' I said, 'No, at the end of the year I always throw them away.'

A shepherd cooked me a pie. It was blackberry and apple. That was nice of him.

Did you know the best-selling DVD this year is Poltergeist? It's flying off the shelves.

I saw this cannibal biting his nails. I said, 'What's eating you?' He said, 'I am.'

I remember when I played Noah in the school play. Ah, the memories are flooding back.

SUNGLASSES

This bloke told me that I smelt like washing powder. It was so bio-degrading.

What do you call a thirteen-year-old with his head chopped off? A guilloteenager.
(That joke was well-executed.)

People often ask me who's my favourite antelope band. It's Gazelles Aloud.

My girlfriend is half-woman, half-fish. I tell you what, it's mermaid all the difference.

There's something about an electric fence that I love but I can't put my finger on it.

When I was 40 I wanted to be an Egyptian. It was a pyramid-life crisis.

I saw a Greek comedian. He had a great sense of humous.

It was non-stop taramasa-laughter.

Ever since I started working in an ejector-seat factory, sales have gone through the roof.

What's a Zulu's favourite chewing-gum flavour? Spearmint.

I'm always dropping cough sweets. I can't hold a Tune. (Tunes were 1970s throat lozenges.)

I tried to surf the internet and I fell off my chair.

LARK DE TRIUMPHE

A lot of my fans are young horses. I've got a colt following.

This bloke said to me, he said, 'If you ever get your own TV show can I appear on it?' I said, 'Be my guest.'

It said a lorry load of tortoises crashed into a train load of terrapins. I thought, That's a turtle disaster.

So I was on the aeroplane and I was sitting next to this bloke who looked exactly like me. I said, 'What's your name?' He said, 'Tim Vine.' I was beside myself.

I passed this man playing 'Dancing Queen' on the didgeridoo. I thought, that's Aboriginal.

Believe it or not there are twice as many eyebrows in the world as there are people.

I went to the doctor's and I said, 'Last night I dreamt I was eating a large marshmallow.' He said, 'Don't tell me. When you woke up your pillow was gone.' I said, 'No, when I woke up one of my large marshmallows was missing.'

So I said to this bloke, I said, 'What do you do for a living?' He said, 'I sell manure.' I said, 'I bet you're rolling in it.'

So I opened the front door when my Dad was in the middle of fixing it and he flew off the handle.

I went to a therapy group to help me cope
with loneliness and no one else turned up.

I had a birthday party. There were so few
people there we had to play Keep the Parcel.

So I went to the barbers. He said, 'Do you
want a crew cut?' I said, 'No there's only me.'

I said, 'Give me a ponytail.' He said, 'Once
upon a time this pony went to the seaside …'

74

Today I met the bloke who invented crosswords. I can't remember his name. It was P something, T something, something something.

I was playing tennis and this 30-foot bicycle went past. I thought that's a long Raleigh.

I was halfway up this mountain and this bloke started attacking me. I said, 'What are you doing?' He said, 'I don't like your altitude.'

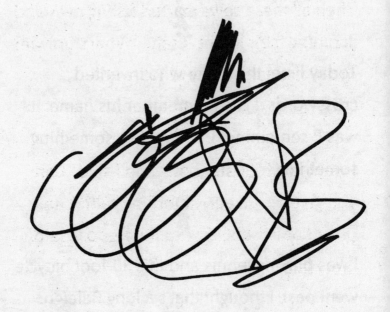

Look I'm doodling
my best all night!

Then all these cows started falling over and scraping their knees. I said, 'What's up with them?' He said, 'They're grazing.'

I went to a four-star hotel and I said, 'Can you give me an early morning call?' The receptionist said, 'Cockadoodledo.' I said, 'Very good.'

So I went down the local shop. I said, 'I'm looking for a sailor with one arm.' He said, 'It's not me. I'm a wholesaler.'

Whenever I get into bed I always think of France because my bedsprings go 'Dordogne'.

So I went to the doctors. I said, 'I've got a rash.' He said, 'I'll be as quick as I can.'

So I was reading this book called *The History of Glue* and I couldn't put it down.

I was born and bred in a bakery and raised in an oven.

STUFFED
VINE
LEAVES.

We even had a pantry. It was a tree covered in pants.

Apparently if you dangle a needle over a pregnant woman's stomach and it goes round and round then it means you're going to have a girl, and if it goes side to side it means you're going to have a boy. And if it gets pulled downwards it means she's going to have a magnet.

Why did Shaggy go to the underwater disco? He likes a Scuba do.

So I went to the pet shop. I said, 'Give me a goldfish.' He said, 'Aquarium?' I said, 'I don't care what star sign he is.'

They say life speeds up as you get older. Which is why you sometimes see a pensioner holding onto a lamp post.

I was invited to a party. On the invite it said 'Look Smart.' So I turned up in a lab coat holding a test tube.

You know when you put on a party invite, 'No Presents, Just Your Presence.' Well, I discovered it matters which way round you put those two words.

I cut a sheep's wool by accident. Shear fluke.

So I went to the baker's. I said, 'The loaf of bread I bought off you that's shaped like Winnie the Pooh has gone stale.' He said, 'Well, we've all got our crusty bear.'

I went to a Middle Eastern shindig. It was a Lebanese-up.

E₁ G₂ G₂

SCRABBLED EGG.

I went to a Far East shindig. It was a Cantonese-up.

I went to a shindig organized by Scrooge. It was an Ebeneze-up.

Have you seen that James Bond film about calculators? *Casio Royale*.

So I said to my mum, I said, 'I've bought you a tablecloth.' She said, 'That's a bit over the top.'

This bloke said to me, he said, 'You're a stencil.' I said, 'Cut it out.'

I've always wanted to be a Hollywood waiter. So I've decided to get a job as a film star and hope a chef spots me.

This bloke said to me, he said, 'I want to explore space.' I said, 'Your mum must be over the moon.'

Since I became a comedian the phone hasn't stopped ringing. It's broken.

This bloke said to me, he said, 'Your answer machine's recorded my voice! Your answer machine's recorded my voice! Your answer machine's recorded my voice!' I said, 'All right, I've got the message.'

So I said to this bloke, I said, 'Where are you from?' He said, 'UK.' I said, 'I'm fine thanks, how are you?'

SPRING BOARD

AUTUMN BOARD

I saw a barrel of oil performing in a comedy club. He was slick but he was crude.

So I bought a rocket salad and it took off vertically.

My dad's in charge of Sunday lunch. He rules the roast.

I used to drive a pizza delivery van. It was a delivery van made of pizza.

I was going to buy some slippers today but then I got cold feet.

Andrew Lloyd Webber's new musical is about a fizzy drink – The Fanta of the Opera.

I went to school in a Wendy house. I found it hard to fit in.

I keep getting deaf threats. Pardon?

Today I mended a violin, I restrung a violin and I polished a violin. Just fiddly jobs really.

CUP & SORCERER

If God had wanted us to re-use everything, he wouldn't have invented peaches.

Apparently stamps are worth more if they've been sent to someone. So I sent all my stamps to someone. And now he's got them.

Do you ever go to McDonalds and when they say, 'Do you want to eat it here or take it away?' You say, 'I want to eat it here,' and you eat your entire meal standing by the till.

92

So I went to the supermarket. I said, 'There's hair on this meat.' He said, 'Let go of my leg.'

I said, 'I wanna ring doughnut.' He said, 'There's a phone in the corner.'

I used to live in a teapot. I know what you're thinking. Poor you.

I once knew a Dutchman with inflatable shoes. One day he went for a run and popped his clogs.

So I ate this chess set and it was horrible. I took it back to the shop and I said, 'That's stale mate.' He said, 'Are you sure?' I said, 'Check mate.'

I said, 'I feel like an indecisive battery.' He said, 'Don't be so negative.' I said, 'But I do.' He said, 'Are you sure?' I said, 'I'm positive.'

So I got home and discovered a burglar pressing one of my shirts. So I punched him, because you've got to strike while the iron's hot.

94

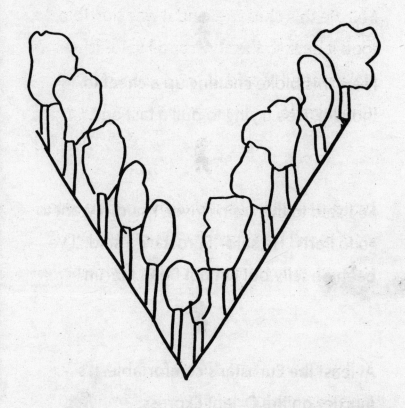

LOOKING UP A TREE-LINED
ROAD FROM THE
WRONG PERSPECTIVE.

I saw this bloke chatting up a cheetah. I thought, He's trying to pull a fast one.

So I said to this train driver, I said, 'I want to go to Paris.' He said, 'Eurostar?' I said, 'I've been on telly but I'm not Dean Martin.'

At least the Eurostar's comfortable. It's murder on the Orient Express.

So I went down the local gym. I said, 'Mr Nasium . . . Can you teach me how to do the splits?' He said, 'How flexible are you?' I said, 'I can't make Tuesdays.'

I love climbing into a small suitcase. I can hardly contain myself.

I went to an Indian restaurant. I thought, *This smells familiar.* Do you ever get that? Déjà Vindaloo?

FUSS POT

The waiter said to me, he said, 'Curry OK?' I said, 'I might do "Summer Lovin" when I've finished this.'

You know those trick candles that you blow out and a couple of seconds later they come alight again. Well, the other day there was a fire at the factory that makes them.

So I went down the local videos shop. I said, 'Can I have *Batman Forever*?' He said, 'No, you've got to bring it back tomorrow.'

I said, 'What about *Another 48 Hours*'. He said, 'Tomorrow.'

I went down the local supermarket. I said, 'I want to make a complaint. This vinegar's got lumps in it.' He said, 'Those are pickled onions.'

I got home and there was a dead chicken flying around the house. So I rang up the vicar. I said, 'Get here quick I've got a poultrygeist.'

So I went to the Chinese restaurant. I said, 'These noodles are a bit crunchy.' He said, 'You're eating the chopsticks.'

100

So I ordered and this duck walked up to me. He gave me a red rose and said, 'Your eyes sparkle like diamonds.' I said, 'Waiter, I asked for aromatic duck.'

I was having dinner with chess champion Gary Kasparov and we had a black and white check tablecloth. It took him two hours to pass me the salt.

He said, 'You remind me of a pepper pot'. I said, 'I'll take that as a condiment.'

RUGBY.

George Lucas has a snotty little brother. He's called George Mucus.

I remember being diagnosed with amnesia. That was a day to forget.

I was in my car doing 30 miles an hour and a friend of mine phoned me. He said, 'I'm 5 miles ahead of you and I'm doing 29 miles an hour.' I said, 'I'll catch up with you later.'

Herod went to the gym every morning. He was fit for a king.

My nephew is a man of very few words. He's six weeks old.

This bloke said to me, he said, 'I've changed myself into a pane of glass.' I said, 'You've made yourself perfectly clear.'

Time for the Bird of Prey Quiz. Fingers on buzzards . . .

DESIGN FOR WORLD'S
SCARIEST ROLLERCOASTER

Do you know the reason why Miss Piggy never got married? It's because she can't Kermit.

So this acorn said to me, he said, 'Whenever I'm underground I head away from the surface.' I said, 'Grow up.'

I tried yo-yo dieting, but it's not easy eating yo-yos. They tend to come back up again.

I saw this bloke laughing like a drain. He was going . . . (Make loud gurgling noise.)

I haven't seen a cowboy film for ages. It's all quiet on the Western front.

If you ever split up with an anchor, let them down gently.

This bloke said to me, he said, 'What's your favourite buzzword?' I said, 'Bzzzzzzz.'

People are always using lingo and jargon. The trouble is, when Lin went she took the jar with her.

Every winter I adjust my car wheels so they don't slip on the ice. Snow chains there.

They say if you're forced to play a musical instrument when you're at school, you're less likely to want to do it later in life. That's true of a lot of things. When I was at school I was forced to stick my head down the toilet.

There's too much wildlife in my garden. I can't get a bird in hedgeways.

THE LIZARD OF OZ

I saw Sherlock Holmes crushing oranges.
I said, 'What are you making?' He said,
'Deduce.'

I saw Watson on the street. I said, 'What's
up?' He said, 'I've been Sherlocked out.'

I went to the Amazon basin. Big taps.

I got stuck in a thick jungle. I couldn't hack it.

This bloke said to me, he said, 'I'm fictional.'
I said, 'Get real.'

In Russia there is a man on trial called Victor Aristov Christov Bannalutech Vich Volstoy Rievenskor. He's trying to clear his name. He'll need a big run-up.

I caught a cold on a carousel. I think there was something going round.

A dandelion. The king of the jungle wearing a cravat.

CHERUBIC CUBE

So I went down the local art gallery. I said, 'You've got a lovely view of the pond from here.' He said, 'That's a painting.' I said, 'Well I'm glad you told me, because I was about to go outside and offer to help those chaps with their cart.'

From now on I'm buying records, not CDs. And that's vinyl.

I used to go out with an anaesthetist – she was a knockout.

If there are any more anaesthetic jokes, I'm not conscious of them.

My local robin has opened a coffee shop in his house. Nestcafe.

I was walking down the street and I passed this man who was shouting, 'Marmite! Nine inches of it!' I thought, That's laying it on a bit thick.

I've taken up speed reading. I can read *War and Peace* in twenty seconds. It's only three words but it's a start.

I went to this church and this bloke threw hot ash on me. I was incensed.

I saw an advert which said 'Television for sale, £1, but it's stuck on full volume.' How can you turn that down?

I'll tell you something that's worth its weight in gold – Gold.

We're told in school that the coldest bit of the flame is the orange bit, which is a bit pointless cos it's still hot. I'm sure when Joan of Arc was burning at the stake no one shouted out, 'Joan, get in the orange bit!'

When I was a teacher I had a nervous tic. Everyone got really good marks.

Everything has changed. Just look at the shops: Toys 'R' Us, Carpets 'R' Us, and there's one near me that sells right-angled triangles – Pythagoras.

I was gonna play my drums today but
somebody stole them. Bongos that idea.

I've got a friend called Peter who changes
his name as often as he changes his shirt.
He's always been called Peter, and he stinks.

I was playing tennis with a napkin and I
said, 'Hey, don't serviette!'

Godzilla fell asleep on the M25 and he's left
a huge tailback.

His school marks
were on the slide.

I bought a dog whistle. It's pointless. Whenever I put it in his mouth he just starts dribbling.

I have got a friend called Lance but I don't see Lance a lot.

I've got a seven-foot fence round my garden and I could see my neighbour walking the other side of it. I said, 'Are you nine-foot tall or on stilts?' He said, 'Both, I'm standing in a ditch.'

So I went to the music shop. I said, 'Can I see your kettle drum?' He said, 'No, but would you like to see my toaster play the nose flute?'

I went down the local swimming baths. I said, 'Your chlorine is really getting up my nose.' He said, 'She's got as much right to be there as you have.'

I get my shoes specially made by a dentist and a carpenter. I have to fight tooth and nail for them.

121

A bit of advice. If a crocodile attacks you, jam a pencil in his mouth. Don't stick it behind his ear.

I did a gig in a zoo and I got babooned off.

I used to be a deep-sea diver but I couldn't stand the pressure.

My banjo said to me, he said, 'Tim I'm leaving you.' I said, 'Why?' He said, 'Because you're always picking on me.'

122

I developed a picture of some cereal. It was a bit grainy.

I think I may be a talented photographer. I took just one photo with my camera phone and it asked me if I wanted to open a gallery.

I saw this man acting suspiciously next to Mount Everest. I said, 'What have you been up to?' He said, '8,000 feet.'

So I was sitting in the launderette watching the washing go round, and I thought I should bring mine in here one day.

Yesterday I cracked a joke. So I can't use it again.

Have you tried that new 007 glue? Bonds in seconds.

I always wear a jacket to chase people. It's my pursuit.

My girlfriend said to me, she said, 'The trouble with you is you've got a glib answer to everything.' I said, 'It takes one to know one.'

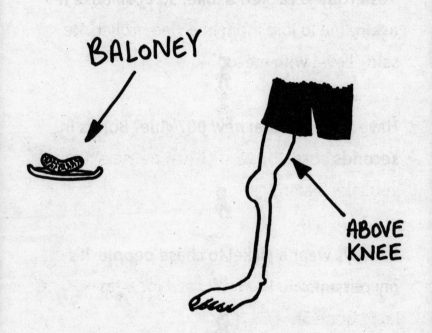

BALONEY

ABOVE
KNEE

I went to the doctors. I said, 'People keep asking me to join them in a steamroller.' He said, 'Level with me ...'

Your next breath of air. I'll just pause while you take that in.

There's a pirate I haven't seen for ages – Long Gone Silver.

The other day I got an invoice for a yak – Buffalo Bill.

Ugly. It's not looking good is it?

The most dangerous winter sport is bobsleighing for apples.

If you're a witch, you've got to make sure you get your five daily potions.

Where does Robin Hood make his own curries? In Sharwood Forest.

I caught an infection at my karate class. It was kung flu.

Scientists have almost invented a supersonic male rabbit. In my opinion, they're just trying to make a quick buck.

The trouble with an all-day breakfast is you've got to eat it so slowly.

So I went to the sweet shop, I said, 'Do you do Twix?' He said, 'I'm quite good at juggling.'

BRITISH AEROSPACE

I went to Pizza Express and there was a sign outside. It said, 'Look out for our new menu.' I walked in and it hit me on the back of the head.

I ordered dessert and he gave me Tiramisu with a blindfolded horse. I said, 'No, mascarpone.'

I went to an airport, I tripped over some luggage and I went flying.

This taxi drove past and it was covered in chilli sauce. It was a mini kebab.

Rugby jokes – it's a nice try.

So I said to this bloke, I said, 'How can I find out when's the next train from London to Glasgow?' He said, 'Why don't you look online?' I said, 'That's a bit dangerous isn't it?'

I've just been on a cycling holiday. It was the most exhausting thing I have ever done in my entire life. I've got to get a smaller caravan.

132

ALMOND-GEDDON

I went to a computer shop and I said, 'Where can I look up information?' He said, 'Yahoo!' I said, 'Do you like that question?'

So this woman began to hover above me and she said, 'Do you want to buy some moisturiser?' I thought, She's having an out of Body Shop experience.

I used to work in a garage which had a jet wash. It was pointless, there was nowhere for them to land.

People used to come in and ask me stupid questions. A bloke came in and said, 'What am I supposed to do with de-icer?' I said, 'Put it on dee windscreen.'

I'm on the Oliver Twist diet. It's gruelling.

Do you know what's in a Waldorf salad? Walls and dwarfs.

So I saw this genie. He said, 'Why am I so frightened?' I said, 'It's obvious. Your bottle's gone.'

So I went to a fancy-dress party dressed as an oven. A friend of mine also came dressed as an oven, and he was really annoyed. He said, 'I thought you said you were coming as a parrot.' I said, 'No, what I said was "I'm coming as a cooker too".'

Then these two sore lips walked passed. I said, 'Hello, chaps.'

LIGHTNING
REACTIONS

When it comes to cosmetic surgery a lot of people turn their noses up.

Do you remember those days when everyone had a tan? – The Bronze Age.

Ladybird contracts. There's a lot of small print.

My dog got a job in a bank. The trouble is, he buried his bonus.

I've got a normal toilet. It's bog standard.

Last night I was eating a pancake and some bloke pushed me. Apparently it was Shove Tuesday.

So I went into my kitchen and I saw a hurricane making a pot of tea. I thought Hmm, there's a storm brewing.

The other day I did a lecture on colourful reefs. A few fish turned up to offer me some coral support.

It's great to see so many familiar faces here tonight. The old two eyes, one nose and a mouth combo. It's still popular.

So I said to this bloke, I said, 'When I took my granny to Egypt she got very confused.' He said, 'Senile?' I said, 'Yes, but she thought it was the Thames.'

People used to call me names at school. They used to say 'Oi! Names! Get over here.'

So I said to this bat, 'How's it hanging?'

A friend said to me, he said, 'I've just removed my son's ears and glued them to his chin.' I said, 'You're spoiling that child.'

I was on a bus late last night. It was just me and the driver. It was really scary because he was sitting at the back with me.

This jellyfish walked into a shop. I thought, He's a slippery customer.

My English teacher brought his dog into lessons. It was the teacher's pet.

I met an annoying peach. He was a pain in the nectarine.

You can say nosey and you can say eerie. But you can't say eye-ee.

So I said to this castle, I said, 'How come you haven't got any water round you?' He said, 'I've been de-moated.'

This bloke said to me, he said, 'I'm never going to use a pen again.' I said, 'Can I have that in writing?'

So I said to this train, I said, 'Why are you late?' He said, 'Sorry, I got sidetracked.'

Mr Pecan, Mr Pistachio, Mr Cashew. What are you, nuts?!

Be careful of the most important buffalo. He's a main yak.

Why do porters get their own loos?

(Tim with boat on his head) 'Do you like my boater?'

This chocolate went past at 100 miles an hour. It was a Ferrari Rocher.

I saw this bloke in a restaurant eating a television. He was having a set lunch.

This bag of rubbish came up to me. He said, 'I'm at your disposal.'

So I went to the Sauna Olympics. It was a proud moment. I was Steam Captain.

The Bayeux Tapestry was bought by a farmer and that's how it got its name. They said. 'Where do you want it?' He said, 'Bayeux.' (Sounds a bit like 'By here'.)

This bloke left a huge lump of plasticine in my dressing room – I don't know what to make of it.

So I said to this Scotsman, 'Did you have spots when you were a teenager?' He said, 'Ach nee.'

I saw this bloke and he was shouting out, 'Lambs for sale. Were ten pounds, now five pounds.' I thought, That's sheep at half the price.

One-armed butlers – they can take it but they can't dish it out.

How come Tarzan was always grumpy? Because he had a chimp on his shoulder.

So I said to Alexander Fleming, the inventor of antibiotics, I said, 'I'd like to meet you on Tuesday.' He said, 'Hold on, I'll penicillin you in.'

An alphabet grenade – if that goes off it could spell disaster.

Velcro. What a rip off.

150

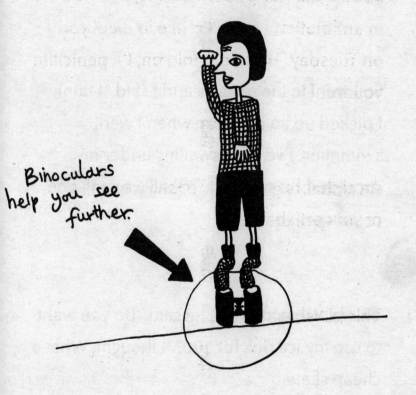

Binoculars help you see further.

So I was mucking about in a lesson and
the teacher made me stand outside. I was
petrified. It was a flying lesson.

So I went to the doctors and I said, 'I think
I picked up an infection when I went
swimming. I've got a swelling under my
shoulder.' He said, 'You're still wearing one
of your arm bands.'

This bloke said to me, he said, 'Do you want
to use my ice rink for 10p?' I thought, What a
cheap skate.

So I was in this horse race and when I got to the finishing line I was hit by an apple seed – pipped at the post.

I'd like to tell you a little bit about my personality. I'm a very private and secretive person ... that's it really.

I'll tell you something that will warm your heart – electrically heated lungs.

It's my girlfriend's birthday today. I bought her a giant helium balloon. That didn't go down very well.

153

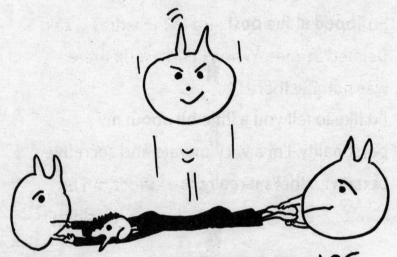

SPACEHOPPER'S REVENGE

So I bought this DVD and in the extras it said Deleted Scenes. When I had a look there was nothing there.

Last night I dreamt I was the author of *The Lord of the Rings*. I was Tolkien in my sleep.

Well, you've got to have a Hobbit.

What's all this fuss about the iPod? It plays 5000 songs in a random order over a one month period. Correct me if I'm wrong but isn't that called the radio?

Do you know what slugs call snails? Gypsies.

I went to this squirrel party. There were hundreds of squirrels there. I said to the squirrel waiter, I said, 'Can I have a bag of nuts?' He said, 'To be honest with you I can't remember where I put them.'

3 weeks old.   2 weeks old.

THE ONE ON THE LEFT
IS THE ELDERBERRY.

This bloke said to me, he said, 'I've got Bubonic Plague.' I said, 'Don't give me that.'

He said, 'I don't like interpreters.' I said, 'Speak for yourself.'

A friend of mine has three legs. He's always one step ahead of me.

This bloke said to me, he said, 'How come your breakfast cereal is bleating?' I said, 'It's the porridge goats.'

I've got really painful fingers. But that's my fault for giving an Indian head massage to a hedgehog.

This Roman emperor said to me, he said, 'What's the weather like?' I said, 'Hail, Caesar.'

Ever since I gave up bread I've lost loaves of weight.

A tortoise on a running machine. Imagine how slow you'd have to set it for him not to fly off the back.

159

I tried to park at Cadbury's but it was choc-a-bloc.

So Pi R squared went round to a circle's house. He said I was in the area . . .

What do you call a little amphibian who never goes out? – Hermit the Frog.

Dear Doctor,
I just wanted to thank you for the pills that you gave me to combat my tiredness. I'm glad to report tha

I was working in a shop and a bloke walked in and started punching everyone. I said, 'Can I help you?' He said, 'It's all right, I'm just bruising.'

Have you heard of that new style of cricket? The only way you can be out is by LBW, bowled or stumped. I know what you're thinking. Where's the catch?

Where does a dog go if his tail falls off? A retailer.

For a long time I thought Perth was where a woman with a lisp keeps her money.

There used to be a band called Half Man, Half Biscuit. But they broke up.

I went to the Royal Albert Hall and it was full of pushchairs. It was Last Night of the Prams.

The Royal Albert Hall is massive, and that's just the hall. You should see the size of the Royal Albert Sitting Room.

163

YAARGH!

SOUNDBITE

My tortoise wrote a book. It was a hardback.

This bloke told me to look at the top of some mountains so I had a peek.

I ran for Parliament once. I had to, I missed the bus.

So I said to Neil Armstrong, I said, 'Is it true the only man-made thing you could see from the Moon was the Great Wall of China?' He said, 'No. If I looked slightly to my left I could see a rocket and a moon buggy.'

I've got an abacus made of Polos on a piece of string. I use it to work out menthol arithmetic.

I saw this cardboard cut-out in a baseball ground. It was the pitcher.

Elton John has a piano in every room of his house. He's even got one in the toilet, but when you leave you've got to remember to put the lid down.

I saw these bits of sheep around the top of a castle. It was the ramparts.

166

I went carol singing last year. I walked round lots of houses with a lantern and nobody gave me any money at all. Still, people are busy at Easter.

My mum takes things literally. The other day I said 'I'd like a cup of tea.' She said, 'Shall I make a pot?' I said, 'Yes please.' And she was gone for half an hour trying to heat up the kiln.

The first colour TV transmission was not entirely successful. They were filming a zebra playing the piano on a giant chessboard.

I once sang in a close harmony singing group. Very close. We used to practice in a phone booth.

Cleopatra used to bathe in goats' milk. She once fell asleep in the Jacuzzi and woke up in a tub of margarine.

Radioactivity. Is that when your radio starts going out and doing stuff?

The trampolening tower of Pisa.

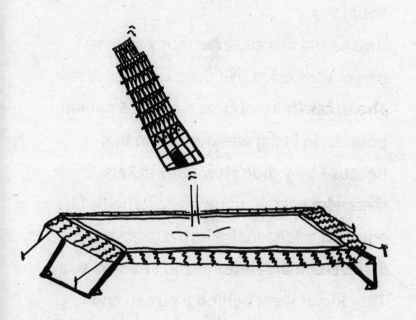

There's a new TV show where you have to dress up as Russian kings. It's called Tzars In Your Eyes.

The Great Train robbers stole £2.5 million pounds. In fact it was more than that because they didn't have any tickets.

So I went to the hospital and I had an X-ray. The doctor went behind a screen and I heard some buzzing. I said, 'Is it finished?' He said, 'No, I'm just having a shave.'

Sandals are called sandals because if you don't wear them on the beach, sand'll get in between your toes.

I made a stew out of a team of rugby players. It was scrummy.

My sister lives in a pillar box. I don't see much of her.

BELLY FLOP WORLD CHAMPIONSHIP

I used to leapfrog over pillar boxes. Last time I did it I broke my nose and two of my ribs, because I tried to leapfrog one of those little square ones stuck to a wall.

So I said to this bloke, I said, 'I was running away from a volcano and I tripped on a rock.' He said, 'Krakatoa?' I said, 'No but I twisted my ankle.'

I asked Linford Christie to buy me some frozen peas and he took ages coming back. I said, 'Where's that runner been?'

I used to want to be a robber in Mexico but they've bandit.

I once danced the tango on an underwater shipwreck. Shoal, shoal, squid squid shoal.

Nelson had five children but only one of them was called Horatio. That's Horatio of one to five.

So I said to this bloke, I said, 'Me and a friend just cycled across the desert with our legs exposed.' He said, 'Tandem?' I said, 'We certainly did.'

VAN GOGH

MASTERPIECE OF CAKE

So I went to the doctors. I said, 'I got hurt in a pillow fight.' He said, 'You've got concushion.'

I saw this film about prehistoric pigs. *Jurassic Pork.*

So I said to this bloke, I said, 'I bet you'd like to see where Dick Turpin lived.' He said, 'Sure would.' I said, 'No, that's Robin Hood.'

I went to a drive-in movie. I didn't see much.
There was a bloke in the front row in a
combine harvester.

The last book I read was an encyclopaedia.
I know what you're thinking. That explains
everything.

If you've got a rabbit it's very bad to carry
them around by their ears. It makes them lazy.

They say all the world's a stage. So how
come we're not all facing the same way?

177

Champagne makes you dizzy but it's cheaper to run in circles.

So I went to the pet shop and I said, 'How much is that doggy in the window?' He said, 'The one with the waggly tail?' I said, 'No, the one next to it.'

This bloke said to me, he said, 'Do you like fencing?' I said, 'Sword of.'

JAM-PACKED

The school I went to was a picture made of coloured paper and seashells stuck on with glue. It was a sixth-form collage.

After I left university I removed one of my front teeth for 12 months. It was my gap year.

I'm glad I wasn't a fly on the wall when they invented fly spray.

Tweet, tweet, tweet. A little bird told me that.

This bloke said to me, he said, 'I'm mute.' I thought, That goes without saying.

Coffee. It's not my cup of tea.

Molecules, atoms, protons, neutrons – I'm rubbish at small talk.

I've got a friend and all he ever wants to do is dress up as a small black insect and live under a rock. He's just a bit anti.

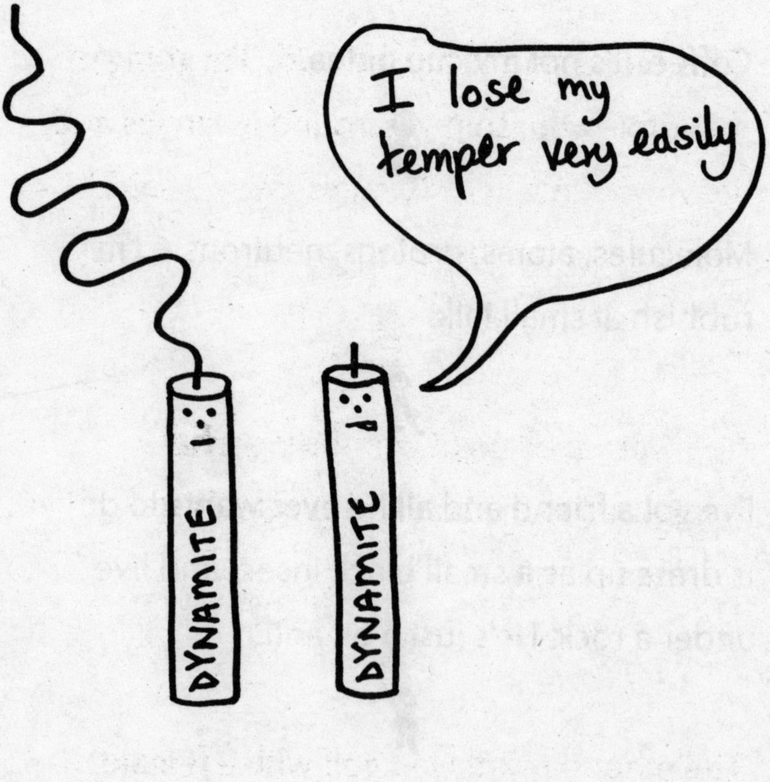
I lose my temper very easily
DYNAMITE
DYNAMITE

So I woke up in the jungle and I was covered in bites. Those tigers.

This bloke said to me, he said, 'I'm going to blindfold you, spin you round in circles and leave you in a field 50 miles away.' I said, 'You've lost me there.'

So I was up all night wondering what happened to the sun and suddenly it dawned on me.

The other day I played golf with a female dog. It was bitch and putt.

Whenever I cry, little wooden huts drop out of my eyes. A lot of tears have been shed.

So I went to the doctors, I said, 'I can hear music at the base of my spine.' He said, 'You've got a slipped disco.'

I said, 'I always put an "s" on the end of words.' He said, 'You've pluralsy.'

I've just eaten an abacus. I've always said it's what's inside that counts.

LINO TAMER

I've planted a redwood in Buckingham Palace garden and I was arrested for high treeson.

I've got a friend who's a pointless beam of light. Laser good for nothing.

I had a polio injection the other day and I can't even ride a horse.

I went to a nightclub during the day and there was no-one there.

Why do you never see an elephant on a bus? Because he's got a massive bum.

Yesterday I fired my cleaner. I'm glad that's done and dusted.

I went to a party in a pendulum. When I got there it was already in full swing.

It's amazing how many poems have been written by a nun. (Oh, it's anon is it?)

HANDLEBAR MOUSTACHE

PEDAL EYEBROWS

Infinity, for ever, eternal, immortal. The list is endless.

I'm terrible at line dancing. I keep going off the page.

My house has just been infested by an Italian sauce. So I rang up Pesto Control.

This bloke said to me, he said, 'Have you ever had a nosebleed in an unusual place?' I said, 'No, it's always my nose.'

I had a haircut at Christmas. All the trimmings.

(NOT QUITE) THE BIGGEST EVER TIM VINE JOKE BOOK

This cat is not Tim Vine